NEXT DOOR NEIGHBORS

a comic strip collection

D1714720

Next Door Neighbors

appears Monday through Friday

on GoComics.com

To Joyce

When I pitched Next Door Neighbors in 2016
to GoComics, I had no idea that six years later I'd still
be chronicling the exploits of Norm Dewey and family.
Yet, here we are, and Norm's still bringing down
the property values in the neighborhood.

So, you're holding in your hands the first volume
of NDN. It contains some of my favorite strips and
story arcs...you have his wife, Jan, the neighbors,
his job, the kids, politics, his mom, Vera, and her cats...
I tried to include a little bit of everything.

Lastly, to my readers—thank you.

Norm thanks you, too.

And you're all invited to his next party.

BYOB

—Pat Sandy, 2022

Carl Ditmer Has anyone looked at the Deweys' house lately?

Joyce Garvey Yeah, it's like the Munsters live there...

Vicki Reynolds They ought to be ashamed...the place is an eyesore...

Herb Ludman I've asked him for years to clean it up, but...

Bob Schmidt And what's the deal with his kid's stupid band? WAY too loud. SMH

Ralph Fernwell And they suck. You forgot that part.

KJ Brimlock The car in the yard is appalling...

Steve Wilton Jeezus, I wish they'd move...

Patty Reigert Is that the guy who mows at 6:30 am?

Ken Floyd Yep. That's him.

Bill Gertz He's such a jerk.

Susan Blick is. We ought to call the and file a for plaint

4-24

6

Bev Roberts Did everyone get their newspaper this morning?

Wilma Doran yeah, I did..

Fred Mullins I got one...

Marianne Dunn I did too... why?

Bev Roberts I didn't get mine...it's almost like someone...you know... took it...

Linda Malone Maybe the carrier messed up... it happens...

Bev Roberts yeah... I guess...just weird, that's all...

4-26

I NEEDED THE COUPONS!

Marianne Dunn Hey...did I ask for your opinion?

Doug Pyle read the Constitution sometime...

Ed Baker I've read it, snowflake...

Joyce Garvey You're such an idiot, Ed...

Sid Bowe voted for Bernie, so I'm ho e runs again...

Wesley ales
W e vo d for

Karen Flanberg Anyone know a decent car mechanic?

Wilma Doran whose dog crapped on our treelawn?!

Howard Mack Apparently, no one cares about HB 345 which calls for the elimination of fundi r the current budge its for various progra benefit busines owner d oth uals th e is o 4-27

Ed Baker Get over it!
Doug Pyle YOU get over it, Ed...

Patty Reigert No one answered my question...

Lonnie Huff what was the question?

Burt Siler selling a 2006 Corolla, b e...best offer.

Carl D an we please change subject? SMH

Ron D ood ails,
libta flake

THE ORIGINAL POST STARTED OUT ASKING FOR TUNA CASSEROLE RECIPES!

M ie eaton l ing for a sitter for next S urday night, $8/hr...pm e...

Myra Fenton What time does the c Center open

John P esist
#notmy dent #imp ch
#g do eidiot lou

JAKE -- I'M SIGNING YOU UP FOR SUMMER DAY CAMP AT THE COMMUNITY RECREATION CENTER...

IT GOES FOR THREE WEEKS AND THERE'S GONNA BE TONS OF COOL ACTIVITIES...

6-5

DOESN'T THAT SOUND LIKE FUN?

IN A WORD-- NO!

HERE-- CHECK OUT THIS BROCHURE...

WELL? HOW WAS THE FIRST DAY OF CAMP?

FABULOUS...

WE ALL HAD TO INTRODUCE OURSELVES, THEN WE SPLIT INTO GROUPS AND CREATED FINGER PUPPET SHOWS...AFTER LUNCH, WE LEARNED SQUARE DANCING...

6-12

...AND TOMORROW, WE'RE GOING ON A NATURE HIKE...

HEY, THAT SOUNDS WONDERF--

PLEASE KILL ME.

WOW--THAT JAKE DEWEY IS A REAL HANDFUL...

HE SURE IS, BUT I'VE PAIRED HIM UP WITH A `CAMP BUDDY'...

`CAMP BUDDY'?

YEAH... PRESTON DOYLE...HE'S IN THE `GIFTED' PROGRAM AT SCHOOL...

I FIGURE IF JAKE IS AROUND A NICE, INTELLIGENT, WELL-BEHAVED KID ALL DAY, IT'S **GOTTA** HELP...

YOU MAY BE ON TO SOMETHING...

6-14

WANNA SEE A COOL PORN APP?

UH...

6-19

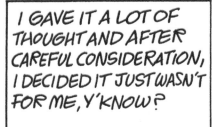

43

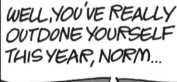

48

I THINK YOU'LL LIKE IT HERE, OSCAR...

WE'VE GOT BALLS OF YARN... BOXES... TREES... TOYS... AND I POST A DAILY SCHEDULE OF ACTIVITIES...

8-14

:GURK!:

THEY'RE ALWAYS A LITTLE NERVOUS ON ORIENTATION DAY!

PFFFT!

SANDY.

HI, MOM--JUST THOUGHT I'D STOP BY, AND--

GOOD GOD, NORM--WHAT A NIGHT WITH THESE CATS... WHAT...A...NIGHT...

THREE OF 'EM WERE SICK, ONE HAD KITTENS AND SEVERAL GOT INTO A SCRAP, BUT THINGS EVENTUALLY CALMED DOWN...

8-20

SO I SPENT THE REST OF THE EVENING WATCHING TV AND FILING THE CALLUSES ON MY FEET...

THAT LAST PART WAS WAY... AND I REALLY HAVE TO EMPHASIZE **WAY**... TOO MUCH INFORMATION...

NOW WHERE DID I PUT THAT PUMICE STONE?

8-21

NORM, IF YOU'RE GOING TO WATCH THE CATS, THEY'LL HAVE TO BE FED, SO HERE'S THEIR SCHEDULE...

THE CALICOS GET FRISKY TENDERS AND ASPARAGUS TIPS, THE TABBIES PREFER TILAPIA WITH RICE PILAF ON THE SIDE AND...

WAIT A MINUTE...THIS IS **ALL** WEEK ?!

THAT'S ONE DAY...

GROAN...

8-23

OKAY, KIDS.. WE'RE IN CHARGE OF TAKING CARE OF YOUR GRANDMOTHER'S CATS WHILE SHE'S ON HER CRUISE...

CLAIRE.. YOU HAVE THE MORNING SHIFT BEFORE SCHOOL...

JAKE, YOU'LL COVER THE EVENING SHIFT AFTER SCHOOL...

WHAT ABOUT YOU, DAD?

I'M COORDINATING!

8-28

WOW--THE BUFFET IS A MADHOUSE...

PUSHY, AGGRESSIVE CROWDS FALLING OVER THEMSELVES TO GET THEIR MONEY'S WORTH...

PLATES OVERFLOWING WITH FOOD...FIGHTS OVER THE LAST SLICE OF PIZZA...THESE PEOPLE ARE RAVENOUS...

IN FACT, I HAVEN'T SEEN THIS KIND OF A FEEDING FRENZY SINCE "SHARK WEEK"!

JEEZUS, NORM...THIS IS **RIDICULOUS**...YOUR HALLOWEEN DISPLAY IS NOTHING BUT A COLOSSAL **EYESORE!**

"EYESORE"?! KIDS **LOVE** THIS STUFF, LUDMAN...IT'S HALLOWEEN FERCRISSAKE... LIGHTEN UP!

BESIDES--WE'RE TAKING DONATIONS AND ALL THE MONEY WILL BE GOING TO A DESERVING CHARITY...

10-15

CHARITY?

THE "DEWEYFUND"...

Bob Willard Has anyone seen Dewey's Halloween display?

Herb Ludman How can you miss it?

Bob Willard What an embarrassment...

Patty Donnell ...guy is an idiot...

Caro... wish ...y'd move...

Ed Baker it does nothing but create traffic problems... people are coming from out-of-town, fercrissake...

Norma Brooks well, it looks trashy...I'm calling the city...

Les Ditman way ahead of you...

Joyce Davids... ...s, he's such an asshole... ...lly wish the gu... ...just m...e ...t

Ken Floyd I saw a tour bus from Pennsylvania drive by...

Barb Wilton my cousin in Indiana heard about it...

Terry Adams it's out of control...

Eric Russell ... lives in Muncie...she ... ...as in the news...r and e...one was laugh... ...t iy a... ...the

MY HALLOWEEN DISPLAYS ARE FAMOUS ACROSS THE TRI-STATE AREA!

Tammy Smith my sist... just called from Pittsburgh... d ...

Otis Vega I'll take that crap down myself...

Mike Mertz he's ... a jerk...

Jack ... re b... g kind...

10-17

103

106

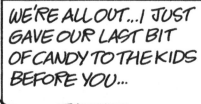

YOU NEVER GOT BACK TO ME ON YOUR NEW YEAR'S RESOLUTIONS...

NO BIG DEAL, THOUGH... I'VE COME UP WITH A FEW, AND YOUR FIRST RESOLUTION IS TO CLEAN OUT THE BASEMENT...

IT LOOKS LIKE **HELL** DOWN THERE, SO YOU'D BETTER GET STARTED-- THIS COULD TAKE A WHILE...

I'LL BE SURE TO GET MY RESOLUTIONS IN ON TIME NEXT YEAR!

1-8

I WENT TO THE LIBRARY AND TOOK OUT THE LATEST OVERSTREET COMIC BOOK PRICE GUIDE...

IF I'M GONNA SELL MY COMICS, I NEED TO BE INFORMED AND GET A HANDLE ON THEIR ACTUAL VALUE...

1-17

IT PAYS TO DO A LITTLE RESEARCH, Y'KNOW?

I'M STILL BACK AT 'WENT TO THE LIBRARY'!

138

HEY, DEWEY-- HOW'D YOUR PERFORMANCE REVIEW GO WITH MR. TOOLEY?

I'LL PUT IT THIS WAY, MYRA -- I STILL HAVE A JOB...

4-17

THEY OUGHTA JUST FIRE YOU, Y'KNOW THAT?

YOU'D MISS ME...

6-21

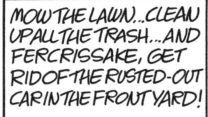

6-27

... COURT IS NOW IN SESSION, THE HONORABLE JUDGE LILLIAN BRECKNER PRESIDING...

SO, MR. DEWEY -- WE MEET AGAIN... WELCOME BACK TO MY COURTROOM...

I HAVE TO SAY -- I GET MORE COMPLAINTS ABOUT YOUR PARTIES THAN ALMOST ANYTHING ELSE...

7-9

PROBABLY FROM PEOPLE WHO WEREN'T INVITED...

TOUCHÉ...

WELP... IT SOUNDS LIKE JAKE'S ALREADY HAVING A BANNER YEAR AT SCHOOL...

HE SET OFF FIREWORKS, SPRAY-PAINTED F-BOMBS IN THE BOYS ROOM...

AND **SOMEHOW**, HE MANAGED TO DRIVE OFF IN THE GYM TEACHER'S CAR... >SIGH<... IT'S ONLY BEEN TWO WEEKS...

9-6

OUR LITTLE OVERACHIEVER!

FRANKLY, JAKE IS PICKING UP RIGHT WHERE HE LEFT OFF LAST YEAR...

AND HE'S BECOME A DISTRACTION, NOT TO MENTION A BAD INFLUENCE ON ALL THE OTHER STUDENTS...

C'MON--AREN'T YOU EXAGGERATING A BIT? HE'S JUST A KID!

HE'S RUNNING A FANTASY FOOTBALL LEAGUE OUT OF HIS LOCKER...

THAT'S RIGHT-- I HAVE TO GIVE HIM MY LINEUP CHANGES...

Made in the USA
Coppell, TX
26 February 2022

74110855R00134